Dirty Pretty Things

Dirty Pretty Things

Michael Faudet

DIRTY PRETTY THINGS

First Edition
ISBN 978-0-473-29950-7

This book is a work of fiction. Names, characters, places, and incidents either are products of the author's imagination or are used fictitiously. Any resemblance to actual events or locales or persons, living or dead, is entirely coincidental.

The Fell Types are digitally reproduced by Igino Marini.
www.iginomarini.com

www.michaelfaudet.com

For Lang,

I write because you exist.

INTRODUCTION

I can write a whole book about Michael, in fact I have written two. I don't think there is anything more to say that cannot be found within their pages. So instead, I will write about a different book entirely. One by Antoine de Saint-Exupéry's known as *The Little Prince.*

In every relationship, there is a defining piece of music, film or literature. One that permeates through the length of every love story.

The Little Prince is significant to Michael and I, in this respect.

Though there have been several books that hold a special significance for us, this particular one trumps them all. The reason why is not a literal one and is difficult to put in words. Perhaps it has something to do with the connection between the Little Prince and the Rose. There is a fragile innocence and beauty to their story that resonates with ours.

Before Michael and I knew each other, we had already shared a similar aesthetic, both in the visual and written form. In fact, it was how we met. He purchased a painting from me and through this transaction, a surprising narrative unfolded. However, though we shared the same appreciation for art, it was our writing that brought us together. Words were our matchmaker.

As we began sharing our writing with each other, we would also share our love of other writers. Because there was such a strong correlation between our words—words that were bittersweet and melancholy—we often fell in love with each other's endorsements.

It was through this exchange that I came to know *The Little Prince*, to rediscover this charming tale as an adult and absorb it once again—not as a child, who can only imagine the exultation and perils of love, but as someone who has loved and lost.

I often think about the love story between the Little Prince and his Rose. It is one that, like Michael, appeared in my life at the exact time when it was the most necessary. I believe it was the same for Michael, for he had rediscovered that long forgotten joy, the moment he pulled his dusty copy of *The Little Prince* from the back of his shelf, to hand to me.

The sentiment of *The Little Prince* can be glimpsed within the pages of my books. It can also be found, scattered in parts of *Dirty Pretty Things*, the book you are holding in your very hands. Between these pages, you will find the remnants of a fierce and unbridled passion, intertwined with the ache of lost love.

I hope you enjoy *Dirty Pretty Things* as much I have. For Michael and I, it has been a labour of love.

Lang Leav, *September* 2014

The Rose

Have you ever loved a rose,
 and watched her slowly bloom;
 and as her petals would unfold,
 you grew drunk on her perfume.

Have you ever seen her dance,
 her leaves all wet with dew;
 and quivered with a new romance—
 the wind, he loved her too.

Have you ever longed for her,
 on nights that go on and on;
 for now, her face is all a blur,
 like a memory kept too long.

 Have you ever loved a rose,
 and bled against her thorns;
 and swear each night to let her go,
 then love her more by dawn.

 —Lang Leav

CAKE

Sex is the cake and love the icing on top.

Away From You

I think of thoughts
    that cannot be,
    no hand can reach
    across this sea,
    the seasons change
    on distant shores,
    from frosty skies
    to sunshine blue,
    as summer's touch
    undresses you—

Reminding me
    of all the things
    I often wish,
    but cannot do.

The Lighthouse

The autumn sun smiled softly across the gentle waves that lapped against the old wooden pier. The lighthouse threw a morning shadow as a magpie's note rang out from the swaying trees.

Dawn's light poured through the dusty wooden blinds and washed over the white linen sheets that lay crumpled and kicked off the bed.

She lay naked, breathless and beautiful. Black hair tumbling across her pert breasts.

'I love our house,' she sighs.

He stares up at the powder blue ceiling, a little dreamy and wet.

'I think this might be a good morning to make marshmallows,' he replies.

Lust

Lust is a lovely word and makes love
so much more interesting

Lost Words

A midnight scribble,
    a morning sigh,
    you watch the words,
    curl up and die.

Madness lives
    inside your head,
    of poems lost,
    and pages dead.

A mind possessed,
    by unmade books,
    unwritten lines
    on empty hooks.

Lips

Kisses dream of lips like yours.

Airplanes

She rode on airplanes and fell asleep in hotel beds. Dreaming of faraway places—writing poetry with her sunset eyes.

VODKA

I couldn't begin to count the countless memories I've lost with each pour of the vodka bottle.

Every one washed away beneath an icy sip or six of liquid forgetfulness. A mind shot to pieces by a forever empty glass.

Yet somewhere hidden within a haze, a fog that descends with the rising sun, a hangover of you remains. Untouched by hands or salty tears that quench this morning thirst.

A fading hint of perfume lost on an empty pillow.

The stray black hair laying alone in the sink.

Your toothbrush dry and carelessly abandoned.

A photograph framed in dust and cobwebs.

Suddenly, I remember all that you were.

She was a ghost of a girl, hauntingly beautiful, wonderfully lost—breaking hearts and crying holy water tears...

A reminder of lips pressed hard against lips.

My hand between your legs, the little pleated skirt hitched up.

Pulling your hair and fucking you hard.

The soft moans and whispered words.

A cat purring, curled up against the tiny rose tattoo on your hip.

Waking up to that smile, the one I fell in love with when the world was just ours.

I open the bottle and shut my eyes.

A twist of fate spilling cold over a lonely glass.

A reminder to forget the forgotten again.

Another day spent slowly slipping away from you.

Reality

Love and loss share the same unmade bed.

Pen Portrait

I watched as you reached for the ice cream.

Standing naked, body pressed up against the humming fridge.

A wispy trail of bluish grey smoke spiraling up from a dying cigarette.

Held precariously in the other hand, ash falling to the floor.

A just fucked wetness between your legs.

Your little smile captured in grainy black and white.

By the click of a camera.

Twisted Trees

A fearsome wind
    cannot compel
    the weakest branch
    to gladly yield.

Yet,
    the faintest breath
    upon your lips—
    and I have fallen
    against my will.

Roses

Roses wear blindfolds,
    Violets crack whips,
    candle wax dripping,
    teeth biting lips.

The Picnic

It was a sticky cotton candy kind of day.

The sun smiling, tickled and teased by wispy white clouds.

Bright yellow butterflies danced a flowery waltz with buzzing bees, while a shadowy wave rippled across the sleepy meadow of lush green.

Its chilly touch, painting tiny goosebumps on pale, winter kissed legs.

Your orange dress hitched up, panties kicked off, my hand exploring the wetness between your thighs.

Our lips thirsty for each other.

Two strangers lost.

In the tangled arms of unquenchable desire.

. . . .

'Why are you crying?'

'I think I've just found the love of my life', she replied.

Lost

Lost is a lovely place to find yourself.

Surrender

Imagine the possibilities,
    of a question posed
    by pretty knees,
    kneeling.

Your eyes cast downwards,
    pleading,
    red lips parted,
    and a mouth
    slowly opened.

The answer given,
    a soft moan,
    swallowed.

Raindrops

We fell asleep as lovers do,
    listening to the raindrops
    pitter-patter on the old tin roof,
    hands entwined and souls
    secretly smiling.

The Blindfold

Sophia opened the pretty pink gift wrapping paper and picked up the black velvet blindfold from inside. Attached was a note written in flowing ink, which read: *Are you ready for instructions?*

She collapsed onto the bed, staring up at the cracks in the ceiling, a quiet smile gently touching each blushing cheek.

THE VISITOR

In soft candle light
    you came,
    a pale white ghost,
    stepping shy
    from shadows,
    coy,
    slipping quietly
    into a restless sleep,
    where all modesty
    and demure
    lay discarded,
    stripped naked,
    by a fantasy
    awakened
    within a dream.

The Race

We ran.

Faces flushed, bare feet sinking into wet sand, our warm breath little clouds of misty white, taken by the chilly morning air.

A single wave broke, sending frothy foam sliding across our ankles, the cold biting deep.

I couldn't catch her.

A trail of flowing red hair unfurling before me, like the tail of a kite cut free from its string.

'Okay, okay...you win', I shouted, slowing to an unsteady walk and stopping, hands on hips, breathing heavy.

She turned around, jogging backwards, her laughter floating towards me.

'You're a wimp, that's what you are and you owe me a hundred bucks!'

We sat.

Eyes staring out to sea, her arm wrapped around my shoulders.

'I love you', she said, kissing me on the cheek.

'I love you too', I replied.

'You know, you can forget about paying me, keep your money'.

'No, you won, fair and square. A bet's a bet and I always pay my debts', I said, my fingers gently brushing away a tangled strand of wet hair from her face.

'Ha! You don't get it, do you? It's me who should be paying you.'

'I don't follow. Well, unless I'm racing you on some beach after a night of a million vodkas.'

Her smiling eyes met mine.

'Do you remember when we first met? What I said to you after we fucked in the dunes, laying on our backs, smoking a joint and searching for shooting stars in the night sky?'

'Not exactly but go on...'

'I told you I wasn't the kind of girl who was easily caught.'

'Yes, now I remember, or I think I do, I was pretty wasted.'

She took my hand and pressed it to her chest. I could feel her heart racing beneath the Mickey Mouse tee.

'You have my heart', she whispered, 'you have all of me.'

Echo

I am hopelessly in love with a memory. An echo
from another time, another place.

Teach Me

Such pretty things
    you said to me—

Unbutton me
    some more.

For I am yours
    to take tonight
    upon this forest floor.

Let's make a bed
    in autumn leaves,
    and leave
    no leaf unturned.

Beneath these trees
    please teach me,
    please—

To learn
    a love
    unlearned.

Bedtime Story

I love the moment when your eyes close
and your lips open in slow motion.

She Said

'Romance is all well and good, but...it's just that I am not in the mood for whispered sweet nothings or your fingers running softly through my hair. What I want, more than anything, is for you to treat me like your own personal sex doll.

Don't kiss me—make me bite my lip.'

Spellbound

The very suggestion
        of your words, she said—
        bind my wrists tighter
        than any rope.

Understatement

'Unbutton, unzip, unclip, untie, undo, undress.'

'Understood', she replied.

ENCORE

I love to watch you touch yourself,
    on rainy afternoons.
    The wandering hands.
    The soft little moans.
    Hips twitching.
    Wet fingers fucking.
    A solo show,
    performed for one.

DIRTY

You make me feel a little dirty, she said, and I fucking love it.

By The Sea

I dreamt of us last night, living in the little stone cottage by the sea, the one you promised me.

Our love held together by wrinkled hands as we slowly walked across ever sinking sands. Each languid step taking us closer towards our very last sunset.

It wasn't until I was fully awake that I truly woke up.

I suddenly realised it's no coincidence the two middle letters of life are *if.*

For every action we make, there is a reaction. The outcome often beyond our control, fragile and fraught with ruinous consequences. Like a soap bubble made real by a gentle breath only to be taken by it.

If you had stayed here, in my trembling arms, would our fingers not be pricked by the thorns of red roses?

And what if our love could have stood up to the storm, standing strong, like our cottage by the sea?

If only...

Curious Girl

She was a curious girl,
    who loved the smell
    of old books,
    chasing butterflies
    and touching herself
    under the covers.

WITHOUT YOU

There is a quiet beauty
    in a miserable grey,
    with leaden skies
    and brooding hue,
    this gentle rain
    a reminder of you,
    tracing silent tears
    on a window pane.

From a changing tide
    to an empty beach,
    a broken wave
    writes a lonely line,
    a crashing metaphor
    captured in time,
    of a memory found
    on this forgotten shore.

Your Smile

Your smile is a beautifully written line
I hope to write some day.

Tongue Tied Love

I cannot speak the words,
    that haven't already been said.
    A well thumbed thesaurus,
    gathering dust,
    inside my head.

It's Complicated

I am here,
 you are there,
 it really is perplexing.

We cannot touch,
 in real time much,
 there's nothing quite as vexing.

Like sex fulfilled
 in bits and bytes,
 and endless late night texting.

Kindness

Do you know what really turns me on?
What I find incredibly sexy? Kindness.

The Mermaid

She came from the ocean,
    this wild girl from the sea,
    her hair flowing southwards,
    she walked towards me.

A west to east smile,
    with eyes steely grey,
    like a storm in the distance,
    rolling in from the bay.

We kissed with the sunrise,
    made love when it set,
    a promise by moonlight,
    came dawn, my regret.

He left for the ocean,
    this boy from the land,
    his spirit soars northward,
    his heart in her hands.

The Kiss

Crashing waves on an empty beach,
    the rhythm of our hearts,
    two drowning lovers lost at sea,
    my lips adrift in yours.

The Muse

Body framed
      with arms outstretched,
      wrists roped,
      and roughly bound.

From a tiny mouth,
      and pretty lips,
      you utter
      not a sound.

I paint with words,
      a canvas stretched,
      laid bare,
      upon the ground.

Perfume

Her perfume reminded me of freshly picked
flowers and sticky candy floss, mixed with
a gentle hint of debauchery.

Stillness

There is a certain stillness, when even the gentle flutter of a butterfly's wing feels like a hurricane.

The moment when crashing waves fall asleep, peaceful, lost to the serenity of salty dreams.

When tall trees stand to attention and every leaf pauses, takes a deep breath and holds it.

It is here, beneath the maddening silence I hear your name.

An echo of you.

Fantasies

Fantasies. Like having your own entertainment channel that you can cut, edit and replay—anytime, anywhere.

Open Invitation

You have such a pretty mouth.
    To feed it only kisses
    would be a wasted opportunity.

Second Chance

We kissed beneath the twisted trees,
    our lips between the stars,
    tiny ripples in a lake,
    this love, once lost,
    is ours.

Words

Words are powerful things. They can break
hearts and make panties wet.

Seduction

The more buttons you undo, she said,
   the faster I become undone.

The Conversation

Let's continue this conversation in bed, she whispered, my legs
can't wait to hear what your hands have to say.

Voyeur

There comes a moment, hidden beneath the gentle moans escaping your lips, where a wet line is crossed. Transforming the act of touching yourself to a whole different level. It suddenly becomes what it really is. Everything you want it to be. Raw, hardcore, legs apart, masturbation.

And as the intensity of the pleasure increases with each repeated circle, the fantasies start to flow. Sticky and swollen. Stretching your imagination and opening you up to your dirty little secrets—

Pulling your hair and fucking you fast.

A tiny mouth opens...

Spasms and shockwaves of pleasure explode between your legs, mini aftershocks rippling over your clenched body, as tight fingers pull on a hard nipple.

You lay beneath the messy sheets, quietly exhausted and smiling.

Undress Me

All that you write,
    you know
    it's not right,
    you move me
    with written suggestion.

I know it's absurd,
    to be undressed by a word,
    write me more
    write me more—
    make me yours.

Rainy Afternoons

I love spending rainy afternoons in bed getting wet.

Words

The words you say,
    so fancy free,
    that fly from lips
    from you
    to me,
    remind me not
    of words I've known,
    when flowers grew
    where weeds have grown.

Touch

I love to trace your pretty lips with my fingers,
and imagine them going down on me.

Raindrops

It was a sparkly raindrops kind of morning—little diamonds falling on leafy green.

Our lips wet, kissing under a tree.

The New York Loft

I watched as your busy fingers moved with a calm state of well practiced precision. The little silver spoon held over a waning candle flame. White chalky dust, turning from a bubbling brown to a clear liquid poison. Drawn carefully through the virgin cigarette filter. Filling a disposable syringe. A poignant metaphor for what was fast becoming your throw away life.

'Please don't, seriously, I beg you...'

She gave me that look. The one that had hooked me all those years ago on that crisp autumn morning. In the forest. Long lashes flickering as her eyes fell into mine. Her reckless body pinned to the soft leafy ground...

I watched her plunge the needle between her toes. Her lips let out a silent sigh. Head rolling back. Red hair tumbling over skinny white shoulders. Nipples poking hard against the black singlet. Legs falling apart. Eyelids closing. Body collapsing. A rag doll falling onto a lonely, unmade bed.

It was a very long minute before the words appeared like ghosts, slipping through the trembling gates of a graveyard.

'I know you love her.'

'Yes, I do, very much', I cautiously replied.

'I know you love her...love her...love....'

She drifted off into a sleep that danced a dangerous pirouette with death. I took it as my cue to leave. Stage exit right. The curtain had finally fallen on this sad little play.

I did love the girl with the crooked black fringe. Who had found her way through the darkness to discover my broken heart. Her tiny, clever hands, stitching it back together. She was my forever girl. The true love of my life. A soul mate.

Closing the bedroom door, I took one last look behind me and then wham. Like a diamond bullet to the brain it hit me. There was a junkie in the room and it wasn't Sophia.

Rendezvous

Red heels
    on a pavement,
    punctuated
    by long legs
    striding
    towards me.

Your lips
    a full stop
    on mine.

Foreplay

Your words touch me in a way I find difficult to
describe, she said, although whenever I read
them it feels a lot like foreplay.

Last Night

Normally I tend to choose my words carefully when it comes to such delicate matters. However, seeing you now, here in the moonlight, all I can think about is pulling your panties down and fucking you with your socks on.

THE SADDEST TRUTH

The saddest truth is realising you have fallen madly in love with what can never be.

Lost Love

I found you,
    hidden by crooked fingers
    of gnarly wood
    and leafy green,
    a pale ghost,
    drifting like morning mist,
    through haunted trees
    and forest birdsong.

You come to me
    in waning moonlight,
    your story told
    on icy skin,
    the pages pale,
    with purple kisses,
    walking barefoot
    and breathless,
    towards my heart.

You found me,
    buried deep
    beneath this earthly blanket,
    of thorny twigs
    and weeping mud,
    two lovers torn
    now bound together,
    in joyful death
    we make our bed.

Room Service

The girl had an impossibly beautiful face, the heady combination of youth and expensive plastic surgery. She smiled as she took my credit card, swiping it with the well practised precision of somebody well versed with stealing ridiculous amounts of dollars from well heeled guests.

'Welcome to the Dakota Hills Hotel, I hope you enjoy your stay with us.'

I took my room key, reached for my lone suitcase and headed for the lift.

'Let me take that for you Sir', said the eager puppy dog bellhop. A hipster looking dude with a coal black designer beard and swept back blonde hair.

Normally I would have said a polite, 'No thank you, I can manage', but I was too tired to argue, sleepwalking through the lobby, looking every bit like a man who has just spent the last 18 hours on an uncomfortable flight from nowhere to somewhere.

A tinny, instrumental version of Royals by Lorde played in the ornate, mirror rimmed elevator. I stared at the numbers, transfixed by every digit change, waiting silently for this part of the nightmarish journey to end. Which it suddenly did with an abrupt stop and the two metal doors sliding open with a hushed whisper.

'I can take it from here', I said, reclaiming my suitcase with one hand and handing over a $10 tip with the other.

'Thank you Sir, replied the beaming bellhop, and if there's anything you need during your stay don't hesitate to ask for me, Gerome...' I didn't catch the rest of his sales pitch, saved by the doors as they slid together just as quietly as they had opened.

My suite was the second doorway from the left. Once inside, room key slid into the slot and low lights coming on, an overwhelming feeling of relief swept over me. Kicking off my shoes I made my way through the little mock lounge to the king sized bed, laid my suitcase on top of it and walked straight over to the mini bar.

Minutes passed as minutes do, drinking slowly from a heavy glass filled with jangling ice cubes and vodka, hypnotised by the streaky night time scene being played outside my window.

Time just seemed to jump cut like a YouTube clip knocked together by a bunch of stoner art students.

I remember taking the body numbing hot shower and slipping into the fluffy white robe that was hung next to another matching one on the back of the door. How I made it back to the bed, unpacked my suitcase and phoned through my late night room service order was anyone's guess.

BBC world news flickered in the background, a story about a train derailment in Madrid washing over me as the second vodka kicked in.

I must have drifted off because the ringing doorbell woke me like a bucket of cold water thrown over a Saturday night drunk.

Pulling my robe tightly around my naked waist I stumbled towards the door, unlocked the chain and turned the handle.

Before I even had time to fully open the heavy wooden door, it was pushed from the outside by a long, black stockinged leg, a room service tray held between two white gloved hands.

The girl flashed a crooked smile and tossed her head back, sending the red ponytail she wore bouncing across her milky white bare shoulders.

'Where would you like this', she cooed, two emerald green eyes sparkling in my direction. It was a rhetorical question. I watched as she set the tray down on the walnut writing desk and hopped onto the bed.

I knew instantly there was something not quite right about this strange scenario being played out in the dimly lit room. She just didn't belong in this movie. Her ivory cream coloured cut off top, short cobweb grey skirt and tattooed arms didn't fit the normal room service uniform script.

'Come up here', she said patting the spare space next to her on the bed.

'Look, I'm not sure what this is all about but I think there has been some kind of mistake.'

A confused and somewhat clumsy cliché retort, but the only one that seemed to make any sense in this moment of fast unraveling reality.

'Think of me as an adventure', she replied, sliding off her red heels.

I didn't really know what to think as my tired eyes fell softly into hers.

'My name is Lucy. Lucy Lockett. You can call me Arousal. All my special friends do.'

'Pleased to meet you Lucy. Do you work for the hotel?'

'Call me Arousal and no, I don't work for anyone. Now, how about you take off that robe and hop into bed. All this chit chat is getting in the way.'

'In the way of what? Listen, I think there has been a serious mix up and you've got the wrong room. I didn't book a hooker and to be perfectly honest I really think you should leave.'

She laughed. Flashing a row of perfectly white teeth. Her mischievous eyes smiling.

'Relax. I don't fuck for money. I fuck for fun, for poetry, for words whispered late at night by strangers.

I felt a curious sense of calm slowly wrapping itself around me like a comfy blanket on a cold winter's morning. A hazy whiteness seemed to fill the hotel room as the walls dissolved away to nothing and I found myself standing naked, my back against a tree in a forest.

Arousal was on her knees, her pretty little mouth sucking my hard cock, eyes looking up at me.

I reached down and took hold of her red ponytail, forcing her head up and down.

My eyes closed as her wet lips worked their magic.

'No, not yet', she said, suddenly stopping and standing up, her lipstick smudged.

She stood before me, bare feet covered by decaying leaves, knees stained by wet mud, breasts bare with dusty pink nipples hard and erect.

Dirty pretty words formed in my head, rearranging themselves into verbal patterns like a kaleidoscope of ever changing verse.

They tumbled from my lips, glowing golden and bright, forming smoky 3D sentences that floated up towards the treetops.

> 'Under a pale pink sky
>   we slept,
>   our eyes wide open.
>
> Awake inside a dream,
>   once dreamt and forsaken.
>
> The time that we lost
>   was not of our making,
>   like a love quickly taken,
>   misplaced
>   and mistaken.'

Arousal spun around and around, arms reaching up into the air, eyes searching the sky, seeking the last wisp of fading words as they got swept away by the breeze.

I could feel the familiar tingling between my legs, the unspoken poetry of longing and desire.

The girl with the red ponytail collapsed to her knees again, eyes looking up at me, back arched and white cotton panties begging to be pulled down.

'Fuck me', she cried, a lone tear running down her blushing cheek.

I gripped her panties with one hand and pulled the crutch to one side with the other. My cock could feel the wetness beneath the soft fabric as it rubbed up against her thighs.

'Fuck me like you hate me,' she purred, her lips curled up into a teasing pout.

The rain came with a whipped up fury of dead leaves and swirling wind.

Three black crows exploded into the angry clouds, wings flapping furiously, punctuating the deafening sound of a million heavy raindrops smashing into the forest floor.

All time seemed to slow down and slowly sink like a drowning child in a stormy sea.

I reached for the handle, opened the door and took the last vodka bottle from the mini bar fridge.

Pouring the contents into the heavy glass tumbler, I caught a quick glimpse of my body reflected in the wardrobe mirror.

A criss cross pattern of bloody scratches stared back.

I could hear the shower running and the echo of a sultry voice singing something sugary and seductive.

Shafts of early morning sun touched the messy sheets that lay strewn across the floor, casting slow dancing shadows over the unmade bed.

It signaled the end of another night and the start of a new adventure.

One that would be tattooed on my heart forever and beyond.

Pressed Flowers

To the quiet one,
    the coy,
    the wallflower.

Her dark circled eyes
    buried in a book.

Hard little nipples,
    dusty pink,
    beneath a tatty
    black singlet.

Those restless legs,
    sprawled across
    a squeaky bed.

Her secrets kept,
    like pressed daisies
    hidden by
    pages read.

Some Days

Some days we spoke about life, other days, we discussed the weather—and whenever we laughed, it was the best sex ever.

Paper Cuts

You tore apart,
    my paper heart
    with words that I was dreading.

Now all that's left,
    of love unsaid,
    is dead and made for shredding.

Like cursed confetti,
    tossed and thrown,
    at a doomed and dismal wedding.

GRATITUDE

Take nothing for granted. Even a rock will eventually surrender
to the sea and love can slip away like sand through fingers.

Wordplay

It is upon
    a pale skin,
    I write
    these words to you.

A story told
    with ticklish pen,
    of all that we
    must do.

To be in love
    with words
    my love,
    and all
    that they depict,
    the dirty
    pretty things
    I wrote,
    each little box
    we ticked.

Unravel

I want to feel your fingers unclip my bra, she said, and unravel
the last thread of decency I possess.

Deception

I fell in love
    with love
    it seems,
    for what was real
    is not.

The lies you spun
    when we begun,
    you thought
    would be forgot.

Time heals all wounds—
    you said to me,
    well this
    I say to you—

The scar I wear,
    I cannot bear,
    for it is
    my heart
    you broke
    in two.

Hentai

We found ourselves, as we often did, sprawled out under the covers of our unmade bed. You, laying on your stomach, laptop open, clicking on Hentai. Me, peering over your bare shoulders, touching a nipple, making it hard, like I always do.

I can hear you breathing, the subtle excitement building with each exhale. My hand reaching down, busy fingers pulling your panties off. A little moan escaping from your tiny mouth.

English subtitles play catch up with the sing-song Japanese voiceover as an animated girl with wide eyes and ridiculously large tits gets fucked up against a wall in a bath house.

Your eyes close for a moment, my wet fingers sliding softly in and out of you.

I slam shut the laptop.

You get up onto your knees, back arched, long black hair slowly falling over your face, my hand pushing your head deep into the pillow.

I get behind you, my cock teasing your pussy and forcing its way in as you bite down on your lip.

We fuck hard and fast. Just how you like it. Your thighs making loud slapping noises against mine.

Suddenly you let out a muffled scream into the pillow, the orgasm catching you by surprise, the spasms gripping my cock tighter as I explode inside you.

We lay on our backs, eyes looking up at the rainbow patterns dancing across the ceiling. Your hand clutching mine.

'Do you want some ice cream?'

I have a habit of asking peculiar questions at times like this.

'Okay', you reply.

You watch as I climb out of bed, tipping the cat off the covers as I reach for my dressing gown.

Before I open the bedroom door, I stop and turn around.

'I love you'.

'I love you too', you whisper, flipping open the laptop.

The Hentai clip starts playing again.

A chubby animated man wearing a white towel is peeping through a crack in the window, watching two naked girls on their knees, scrubbing the wooden floors of the bath house with wire brushes.

You pause the scene, your smile reflected in the screen.

Waiting for me to return.

Ruin Me

I'm the kind of girl who has a restless mind and impatient legs...

I watched as her fingers nervously flicked the well worn elastic of her white cotton panties.

I want you to ruin me.

THE WISH

Every time you take a sip,
     your lips wet with wine,
     I wish I was that glass.

Deeper

Every time you open your eyes I fall deeper
in love with the story they tell.

Sundays In Bed

The lazy tide rolled in like a snail smoking weed.

Much to the amusement of the crooked trees that waved a leafy wave and poked fun at the salty breeze that giggled back.

Even the fish, little iridescent rainbows, smiled.

Seduced by a psychedelic sun that teased and tickled its way across the laughing orange carpet that was the sea.

Sparkles.

Little diamond fragments shone from green fingertips.

And still the rain fell.

While she collapsed under the crumpled sheets.

Wet and wetter.

He on his back, exhausted and smiling.

Another afternoon in bed.

Well spent.

Writer's Block

There was something quite perverse about my love of crisp, cold days, especially the ones touched by a weak watery warmth, which spilled down from skies of winter blue.

Perhaps it was the remoteness of being that appealed to me.

Sitting in an empty park, surrounded by the towering trees, bare and lonely, their leaves long departed and now left decaying on the chilly ground.

Even the odd flap of wings from startled sparrows, darting between bare limbs and twisted branches did little to interrupt the stillness of this solitary moment.

Where I found myself, as I often did, writing endless poetry in scrawly pencil strokes.

My fingers frozen, as the faint grey words fell upon the pristine pages of a battered, leather bound journal.

Every sentence formed, a furrow ploughed across an empty field, where seeds refused to grow.

I remember once, many years ago, finding myself transfixed and strangely hypnotised by the mechanical whirring of an automata.

Two metal monkeys, grimaced faces covered in speckled paint and tuffs of tatty black hair, sitting opposite each other, weary combatants dueling across a tired looking wooden chessboard.

I watched as their arthritic paws moved the pieces with robotic precision, playing the same game over and over again with identical conclusion.

After every checkmate, they reset the pieces to start playing again, only stopping to be rewound by the turn of an ornate brass key.

A beautiful exercise in futility, repetitive and strangely cathartic.

Like a pencil driven between the blue lines by a driver with no clear direction in mind.

'The more you write, the more you write.'

I can't recall who said that to me, but the words stuck. An inky stain, dark black and impossible to remove.

A throaty bark from a panting dog broke the silence.

Its muddy paws kicking up leaves, tail wagging, chasing a faded green tennis ball thrown by a loved up couple, wearing his and hers matching blue anoraks.

I watched them walk away, a trail of faint laughter clinging to a tangled thread of wispy breeze. A distant memory left behind with every step and fast unraveling.

A last kiss stolen from Lucy's tear stained lips. Salty and unforgiving.

Her hand slowly slipping away from mine as we sat on this very bench.

'I love you, but, I just can't live with you anymore', the words she wrote with a voice frail and broken.

A miserable ending to our magnificent love story.

One that my pencil still refuses to write to this day.

A Final Kiss

May my last breath,
    be it faint,
    and whisper thin,
    meet death quietly.

A final kiss,
    buried gently,
    within the warmth,
    of the only lips,
    I ever lived,
    to truly love.

Fireworks

She had a mind like a box of fireworks and hands
that played recklessly with matches.

The Apple Orchard

He floated upon a gentle sea of rippling green.

Where little yellow butterflies danced drunk pirouettes on the windy stage.

Reading the words written by fluffy white poets who wrote ever changing prose across an endless blue page.

'Apples are funny things,' he said. 'You can never be sure of what you are getting until you take that first bite.'

His hand reaches slowly for the half empty vodka bottle.

'This afternoon I discovered an apple so wonderfully perfect, I wouldn't be surprised if it came from the outstretched hand of a wicked old witch.'

She pulled up her white cotton panties, brushing an ant from a grass stained knee.

'I've been called many things before but never an apple', she laughed.

Stormy Weather

We made love on stormy summer nights.

Our kisses wet and furious like rain running wild across the naked ground.

Her gentle moans lost in the rumble of thunder.

I Love You

The most beautiful
      sound in the world to me
      is not forest birdsong
      or babbling brooks
      or even the ringing
      of church bells.

It's hearing you
      whisper, 'I love you',
      over and over again.

Lollipops

Yellow taxi tyres screech to a sudden stop. A door slams shut. Steps stirring up swirling pavement puddles. Tripping over rusty tin cans in the cobblestone lane.

Anticipation finally arrives in the shape of a corner shop.

Rain streaked heart shaped windows. A seductive wink from a sultry flashing neon sign. *Lollipops,* meticulously written in silver scripted, letterpressed letters. A place where generous sprinklings of sugary sex are swapped for a handful of crumpled dollar bills.

A promise becomes permission.

I walk you slowly through the red leather door. Little kitten heels and long white socks. A cotton candy smile. Nipples fighting hard against the tight tunic top that I bought you last summer. A ridiculously short, grey pleated woolen skirt.

Tired candles yawn. Casting cryptic shadows across the pink and cream striped hallway, where glory holes wait.

You kneel down.

I push the shiny black token into the slot.

You look up at me. Eyes begging softly.

I lean down and quietly whisper words, best left unsaid.

A thick hard cock suddenly appears from a hole in the wall. Beautifully gift wrapped in black cellophane and a red velvet ribbon bow.

Furtive fingers reaching out. Silently untying.

As tearing turns to torn, a tiny mouth opens. I gently lift up your skirt from behind. A little wet patch appears on your pretty panties. I feel myself harden. Watching your hungry lips devour and swallow.

Your birthday present.

Sunday At The Cemetery

*It has been said, that to wear a scarlet dress in a
cemetery can attract the spirit of a lover long dead.*

. . . .

If you were taken from me,
    from this place I call our world,
    I would not cry,
    or even sigh,
    wring my hands,
    or wonder why.

Instead you'd find me waiting,
    ever by your side,
    every single second,
    this rule I do abide.
    Whatever did this girl possess?
    The question they will pose,
    to make her wear the scarlet dress
    and hold a ruby rose.

If you were given to me,
    from this place I call your heart,
    I would not cry,
    or even sigh,
    wring my hands,
    or wonder why.

Fate

I never truly believed in fate until your lips met mine
and convinced me otherwise.

A Parting Gift

I cannot sleep,
    I cannot cry,
        I cannot even wonder why.

You broke my heart,
    will I be missed?

Red ribbons wrapped
    around my wrist.

Perfect Timing

Sometimes you make me feel like a clock perched on a dusty shelf, she said. Counting down the hours, the minutes and seconds until we meet again.

And when we do, the hands become my legs.

Forever stuck on 4.40pm.

SMITTEN

Oh to be smitten,
    tangled
    by silly cuteness,
    like a ball of red wool,
    chased by a kitten.

My lemon meringue pie,
    sugary sweet,
    with a trace
    of playful sour.

Let's catch
    our summer butterflies,
    blue skies,
    radiant
    above.

Two foolish fools
    falling—
    in love,
    with love.

Sunday Enlightenment

I am afraid of the dark, she said.

I am your touch, he replied.

The Forest

Beneath a canopy of fluttering green we lay, eyes closed, backs pressing against the forest floor of fallen leaves and crooked twigs. A gentle wind whispered sweet nothings, a voice laced with shrill birdsong and creaking branches.

I could hear you breathing, your hand entwined in mine. The memory of your scent still wet upon my lips.

'Close those beautiful eyes and lift up your skirt ever so slowly. Show me where you want to be touched.'

It almost seemed a lifetime ago when our eyes first met.

Sipping from champagne glasses and staring across a freshly cut lawn of emerald green littered with well heeled drunks and lipstick stained cigarette butts.

I watched as you floated towards me like a lost feather in a careless breeze.

A black bra strap fallen from a milky white shoulder.

Lips painted crimson.

Afternoon sunshine curled up on a bed of flowing black hair.

Your hand silently taking mine.

Leading me towards the forest with barely whispered words.

'Make me wet. Make me moan. Make me yours.'

I heard the rustle of autumn leaves.

My eyes opened to a setting sun through the forest canopy.

Turning my head I could see you standing.

Adjusting the little blue cotton pleated skirt.

One white sock missing.

Knees dirty.

I find the idea of getting down on my knees terribly exciting, she said, now, make me beg for it.'

I lit a cigarette while my mind drifted between the now and then.

The blue smoke forming a question mark, punctuating the crisp afternoon air.

'I don't even know your name', I said.

'Does it really matter', she replied, placing the crumpled panties into her black leather handbag.

Text Received 28-03-2010

Inside forest. On a muddy track that runs through it. One slip and you're falling into the gully. Silence punctuated by bird song. Green everywhere. We should come and explore in the morning. We will have to be careful. Cover your mouth as you orgasm. Sound travels here.

Chocolates

She was the kind of girl
    who loved to stretch out
    under the sheets,
    eating chocolate,
    reading books
    and fucking on
    rainy afternoons.

SUNDAY EPIPHANY

Suddenly I landed.
    The wind knocked out of me.
    Heavy gasps.
    Breathing in slowly.
    Fingers checking.
    Nothing broken.
    Eyes closing.
    You smiling.
    Me realising.
    How hard I have fallen—
    in love.

Forbidden Love

It cannot be—
    she said to me,
    the end
    is not my making.
    To keep apart,
    two lovers hearts,
    is another's undertaking.

This might be true—
    I said to you,
    but it is they
    who are mistaken.

For where there's a sun
    you'll find a moon,
    and neither
    can be forsaken.

Snow Storm

Outside, the snow continued to fall, whipped up by a swirling vicious wind that knocked on the frosty windows and rattled the old wooden door.

Inside the tiny stone cottage, it was a different story.

Flickering flames from a glowing fire cast leaping shadows, which danced like drunk ballerinas across the cobwebbed walls.

Your hand reached for the vodka bottle.

Mine stroked a thigh which begged to be touched, caressed and kissed.

'I'm feeling tipsy', she laughed, filling her glass to the brim, the contents overflowing, forming a small puddle that quickly soaked into the wine stained rug.

'Would you like to hear a story?'

'Of course', she replied, pushing my hand under her skirt.

'Well, once upon a time, when I was living in Berlin...'

'Stop right there, she said, I've heard this one. Remember? The gypsy girl who stole your heart and keeps it in a golden cage. You always repeat yourself when you're drunk.'

She was right. I had told her the story, as I had the many others who had drifted into my life and melted away, like delicate snowflakes captured by a winter sun.

'Here, drink this and forget about it. I don't care if you can't love me. I honestly don't.'

I took the bottle from her outstretched hand and swallowed two generous swigs, a warm river running down my throat.

Emily smiled and stood up, her gorgeous green eyes twinkling in the darkness.

'You know what I want? More than anything right now', she said, hitching up her skirt to reveal the black lace panties with a pretty red bow, 'I want you to fuck me like you fucked that gypsy girl.'

I put the bottle down and pointed to the bed that sat waiting in the corner of the room.

'Why do we need a bed when there's a perfectly good table right here?'

I watched as she climbed onto it, kicking a chair over with a bare foot as she turned over, pressing her back down on the hard wood, legs slowly spreading wider.

'It's time you wrote a new story, one I haven't heard', she whispered.

Strawberries

She was a curious girl, a wanderer, who spent her summers chasing fluttering pieces of prose and eating strawberries.

Bitter Sweet Love

To slap you,
    is to touch you.
    Scream for mercy.
    Beg for more.

To bite you,
    is to kiss you.
    Tied and tethered,
    on the floor.

To loath you,
    is to love you.
    Pretty princess.
    Dirty whore.

True Love

When you're in love, truly in love, you never have to question it.

Confession

Sticky fingers
    on sugary lips;
    a criminal returns
    to the scene
    of a crime.

A wry smile,
    betrays her innocence;
    a signed confession
    witnessed by
    blushing cheeks
    and auburn hair.

Naked guilt,
    a punishment dealt;
    over a wooden table,
    where a jam donut
    is noticeably absent.

Virgin Snow

Your scream
     startled birds,
     rising up from
     naked trees,
     laid bare
     by winter's breath.

Little clouds
     of spoken mist,
     from the lips
     of lovers lost,
     fade to nothing.

Pretty knees
     turn to icy blue,
     on frozen sheets
     of brilliant white,
     in a bed
     of falling snow,
     stained red.

WHISPERS

Some nights I close my eyes and imagine feeling your lips on mine, your whispered words slowly pushing my legs apart.

Uncharted

Think of me as an uncharted map.
I want your hands to explore every single city, town and village.

Dying Flowers

Love came
    as it often does,
    all smiles
    and fragrant flowers,
    but when it left
    it left behind,
    the fallen petals
    of what was
    ours.

Kiss Me

Yes, I dream of many things, she said, and the thought of your hand between my legs is just one of them.

Now shut up and kiss me.

PRETTY TORMENTS

I love,
> how you like
> to tease.

Slowly crawling,
> while your legs
> do the talking,
> with knees
> that blush,
> on wooden floors.

Dropping a pencil,
> and picking it up.

Overwhelmed

I know I shouldn't be telling you this, she said, but I have
an overwhelming urge to fuck you—right here, right now.

Ice Cream

Would you prefer chocolate or strawberry ice cream?

I'm surprised I even have a choice, she replied.

You don't—

Now close those eyes and open your pretty mouth.

Changing Tides

Sometimes if
  I stop
  to think,
  this life
  we share
  could drown
  and sink,
  beneath
  the waves—

I contemplate,
  about the love
  we do
  create.

Good Night

May you fall asleep in the arms of a dream, so beautiful,
you'll wake up crying.

The Thief

It wasn't right,
    you know it's wrong,
    the heart you took,
    did not belong.

But now it's gone,
    it's yours to keep,
    for another's loss,
    is theirs to weep.

Red

She was obsessed with the colour red,
    this dangerous girl with scarlet lips.
    Her reckless kisses written in blood
    upon a page I could not turn.

Stars

Magic tumbled from her pretty lips and when she spoke the
language of the universe—the stars sighed in unison

Wet Dreams

Such a gorgeous tangle
    your legs in mine
    a fantasy is sold.

Our outstretched arms
    explore the charms
    of desire and sex
    well told.

We live this dream
    of moans and screams,
    a life in bed
    all spent.

Spring

She wore the scent
    of early spring
    on her delicate neck
    and every kiss I stole
    tasted of bright yellow flowers
    and buzzing bees.

Melancholia

I am alone,
    love passes by.

Crying tears,
    I wonder why—

I cannot find
    what others found.

First Kiss

The first kiss is the last to be forgotten.

The Drowning

I fell into a sea of tears
    and sank beneath its waves,
    each breath I lost,
    became the cost,
    I paid for wasted years.

To sink or swim
    a question posed,
    an answer lost within,
    a sorrow kept,
    drowned by regret,
    I cry for you again.

Desire

I never understood desire
     until I felt your hands
     around my throat.

Suggestion

I love thinking about your mouth on my nipples and your hand up my skirt, she said, in fact the very suggestion of you makes me want to pull my panties down.

Playing With Matches

I lit
    this fire,
    burning fierce,
    and all consuming.

My desperate tears,
    useless,
    against flames that leap,
    turning
    my breaking heart
    to blackened cinders.

Lipstick

Grab my hair and bring me to my knees.
Smudge my lipstick and ruin my pretty lips.

My Girl Who Writes

I watch you write,
    my love, my life,
    my start of everything.

Each little sigh,
    a pen run dry,
    another painful page
    begins.

Your fingers bleed,
    I do concede,
    for a sentence
    of your making.

To which you say,
    on sunshine days,
    it is for words
    my heart is breaking

A Question For Anna

Do you know what a palindrome is Madam?

Bonsai

What could be
  a love so fierce,
  in your hands
  so gently trimmed.

Each little cut
  you take with caution,
  a love suspended
  but never grown.

Book

Put your hands on my knees, she said, and think of me as a book you've been dying to read.

Her Little Secret

I know it's wrong,
　　　but the very thought
　　　of your hands,
　　　reaching up under
　　　my skirt,
　　　and touching me,
　　　makes me blush
　　　in all the right places.

Love Story

To read in books
    of love well told,
    leaves nothing
    in the meaning.

For the love
    we have
    is barely held,
    between pages
    of our reading.

TRUE LOVE

True love is elusive, she said, sometimes I think it's as rare as a red moon on a cloudless night.

First Love

Petals unfurl
    from a delicate flower,
    closer to picked
    with each
    passing hour,
    losing the I
    and gaining
    an our.

HYPNOTISED

I am hypnotised.
   Sleepwalking to the rhythm of your words,
   Never wishing to wake—

Love Letters

The kind of love letters I write are the ones
    you read in bed, stretched out under the sheets
    with one hand beneath your legs.

Dreams

She turns her mind
    to countless things,
    then back again
    where it begins.

This restless urge,
    and all it brings,
    to be someone—
    to do something.

The Gift

Her eyes were beautifully gift wrapped;
    long black lashes of velvet ribbon—
    and every time she opened them,
    it felt like Christmas.

Poetic

Now's not the time to be poetic, she said, just pull my panties down and do me up against this tree.

The End

I could taste
     the sting of whiskey
     on your lips,
     a final kiss,
     before we said
     our last goodbye,
     without a word
     being said.

Acknowledgments

To my mum and dad, for all the freedom, love and support you've always given me.

My sister, Genevieve, who sacrifices so much of her life to help others. Respect.

My grandparents, who spoiled me in the nicest possible way.

To my ridiculously clever son, Oliver. I love you more than all the words in the world.

My beautifully mad friends, (you know who you are), thank you for the wine, conversation and endless laughter.

And last, but by no means least, a special thank you to my readers, for your continued support and wonderful kindness.

About the Author

Michael Faudet has done many interesting things.

Most notable was enjoying an eighteen year career, working for arguably one of the most creative advertising networks in the world.

During his time at DDB, he has held the positions of Director on the Australian management board, Managing Partner in New Zealand and Executive Creative Director in the Auckland, Sydney and Melbourne offices.

He has tutored extensively, guest lectured at universities, sat on many industry judging panels and has spoken at creative conferences around the world. Michael has also won numerous international awards in some of the most prestigious advertising shows.

In 2013, he decided to walk away from advertising to focus on his own creativity and writing. He also helped launch the international best seller, 'Love & Misadventure' by author Lang Leav.

Michael's poetry and prose explores the many facets of love and relationships. His whimsical and sometimes erotic writing quickly went viral and continues to attract a growing cult following of readers from around the world.

His first book, *Dirty Pretty Things,* is a collection of poetry, prose, quotes and little short stories. He is currently working on his second book, a modern day fairytale with dark, gothic undertones.

When he is not writing, you'll find Michael sharing a bottle of wine with his poet girlfriend, Lang Leav, in their little house by the sea.

INDEX

Join Michael Faudet on the following:

Facebook   **Tumblr**   **Twitter**   **Instagram**

POSTED POEMS

Posted Poems is a unique postal service that allows you to send your favorite Michael Faudet or Lang Leav poem to anyone, anywhere in the world. All poems are printed on heavyweight art paper and encased in a beautiful string tie envelope. To send a Posted Poem to someone special visit: langleav.com/postedpoems

CPSIA information can be obtained at www.ICGtesting.com
Printed in the USA
BVOW08s1818130915

417248BV00002B/9/P